*V*isiting the *P*ast

The Pyramids

Haydn Middleton

Heinemann
LIBRARY

www.heinemann.co.uk/library
Visit our website to find out more information about Heinemann Library books.

To order:
☎ Phone 44 (0) 1865 888066
▤ Send a fax to 44 (0) 1865 314091
 Visit the Heinemann Bookshop at www.heinemann.co.uk/library to browse our
catalogue and order online.

First published in Great Britain by Heinemann Library, Halley Court, Jordan Hill, Oxford
OX2 8EJ, a division of Reed Educational and Professional Publishing Ltd. Heinemann
is a registered trademark of Reed Educational & Professional Publishing Ltd.

OXFORD MELBOURNE AUCKLAND JOHANNESBURG BLANTYRE
GABORONE IBADAN PORTSMOUTH NH (USA) CHICAGO

Designed by Visual Image
Illustrations by Paul Bale
Originated by Ambassador Litho Ltd
Printed by Wing King Tong in Hong Kong/China

ISBN 0 431 02784 6
06 05 04 03 02
10 9 8 7 6 5 4 3 2 1

British Library Cataloguing in Publication Data

Middleton, Haydn
The Pyramids. – (Visiting the past)
1. Pyramids – Egypt – Juvenile literature 2. Egypt – Antiquities – Juvenile
   literature
I. Title
932

Acknowledgements

The publishers would like to thank Peter Evans for permission to reproduce all photographs with the exception
of the following: Christine Osborne Pictures: p.12; Haydn Middleton: p.13 (bottom), p.21 (top);
Scala Art Resource: p.11 (bottom).

Cover photograph reproduced with permission of Peter Evans.

Every effort has been made to contact copyright holders of any material reproduced in this book.
Any omissions will be rectified in subsequent printings if notice is given to the Publishers.

Any words appearing in the text in bold, **like this**, are explained in the Glossary.

Contents

Wonder of the world

A sk anyone, anywhere, what they think of when they hear the word 'Egypt' and they will probably say 'The Pyramids'. People have been saying the same thing for almost 5000 years. Not long before the birth of Christ, writers made a list of the Seven Wonders of the World. These were the most marvellous statues, gardens, temples and other buildings of ancient times. Even then, the oldest wonder was the Pyramids at Giza – a place on the edge of the desert just west of Egypt's modern capital city, Cairo. None of the other six wonders of the ancient world survive in all their glory. The Pyramids do. 'Time laughs at all things,' says an Arab proverb, 'but the Pyramids laugh at time.'

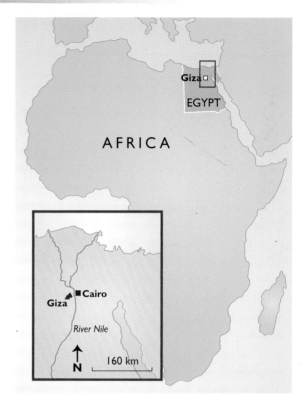

The people of ancient Egypt lived along the River Nile in North Africa. The Pyramids at Giza are just three of around a hundred that were built during the Old and Middle Kingdoms. All of them stand to the west of the River Nile. That was where the sun went down or 'died' each day. So the ancient Egyptians believed this region was a land of the dead.

The ancient world's largest and most famous sculpture stands at Giza too: the Sphinx. Originally carved from a single block of limestone, it dates back to Egypt's Old Kingdom, but historians and **archaeologists** still argue about what it was made for.

Pharaohs' tombs

There are three great pyramids at Giza. Elsewhere in Egypt there are over 90 more, although none can match the two tallest pyramids at Giza in height. Each one was a tomb specially built for a **mummified** Egyptian king or '**pharaoh**'. Some of these pharaohs ruled over what is known as the **Old Kingdom** of ancient Egypt – a period that lasted from about 2575 BC to 2130 BC. Others ruled over the **Middle Kingdom**, which ran from about 1938 BC to 1600 BC. By the time of the **New Kingdom** (about 1540 BC to 1075 BC), pharaohs like the famous Tutankhamun were buried in secret rock tombs, not pyramids.

But although the immense Pyramids at Giza are so well-known, there is still an air of mystery about them. We cannot be certain why the ancient Egyptians gave them this particular shape. Nor are we sure exactly how they were built. Guessing at the answers makes a visit to this awesome site even more enjoyable.

A pyramid was more than just a royal tomb. It was also meant to show how mighty the pharaoh had been during his earthly life. His god-like powers were supposed to live on after his death and continue to benefit the people of Egypt.

The earliest and most northerly pyramid at Giza was built for King Khufu. Often called the Great Pyramid, it is actually higher than that of King Khafre next to it, but Khafre's was sited on slightly higher ground. Around AD 1800 some French scholars studied the Pyramids at Giza, and claimed that a wall could have been built right around France with all the stone used in the Pyramids!

Pyramids plus

Built on a high **plateau**, the three Pyramids at Giza dominate the horizon for miles around. But they were never intended to stand alone. Each pyramid was part of a **complex** of other structures. Many of these have also survived. Most are now in ruins, however – worn away by age, or dismantled by people who used the stone to make new buildings elsewhere.

Main pyramid

Funerary temple

Surrounding wall

Temple courtyard

'Baby' pyramid

Causeway (actually much longer)

Lower temple

We cannot know precisely what an ancient pyramid complex looked like. The drawing above is based on what we can work out from **archaeological** evidence. The main pyramid area was probably surrounded by a high wall. Inside it was a **funerary** temple – with a courtyard where **offerings** such as food could be left for the dead **pharaoh**. Perhaps there were one or more 'baby' pyramids too, where relatives of the pharaoh may have been buried. Then a long ramp called a **causeway** led down from the funerary temple to another holy place, called the valley temple. This was probably where the pharaoh's body was brought to be **embalmed** before it was entombed.

This is all that now remains of the large funerary temple on the east side of the third pyramid at Giza, built for King Menkaure. In death he became a god, and the living went on worshipping him in this temple. The pyramid rising up just beyond it belongs to King Khafre, the father of Menkaure.

Fixed positions

Each Giza pyramid once had a complex. To the east and west of the Great Pyramid of King Khufu, there were also large cemeteries for many high-ranking Egyptians who lived in the centuries after him.

The entrance to each pyramid faced north, parallel to the life-bringing River Nile that flowed northwards a short distance away. Both temples were always built to the east of the pyramid. There they would catch the rays of the rising sun. Just as the sun rose or was 'reborn' each day, so the dead pharaoh was supposed to be brought to life after being entombed. By living on **eternally**, he could keep watching over his former subjects – and make sure they continued to enjoy 'Maat'. This meant peace, justice, truth, order, trust and harmony between heaven and earth.

To the south of King Menkaure's Pyramid stand three smaller pyramids. Known as the Queens' Pyramids, they were never finished. They may have been the final resting-places of three of Menkaure's wives. The name of one wife was Khamerernebty II.

A glimpse inside a private tomb to the east of the Great Pyramid. Leading Egyptians wanted detailed evidence of their lives on earth to be shown in their tombs. The resulting **reliefs**, statues and **hierogylphic** writings are vital sources of information on what people looked like and did nearly 5000 years ago.

Shipping stone to Giza

Huge amounts of stone were needed to build the Pyramids and their **complexes**. Most of the **quarries** were nearby, but some of the material was brought from Aswan, hundreds of miles away. How was it all transported to the site at Giza, when the ancient Egyptians had no wheeled traffic? The answer is by water.

The vital Nile

Egypt was, and is, an **arid** country except for a strip of land to either side of the River Nile. During the season of 'akhet' (mid-July to mid-November) the river flooded over this strip, making the land **fertile** at the hottest time of the year. During 'peret' (mid-November to mid-March) the river returned to its bed, leaving waterlogged fields that the farmers could work in. The dry season of 'shemu' followed (mid-March to mid-July), with the river at its lowest level, and the parched soil cracking for lack of water. This was the time when the crops of grain and **flax** were harvested.

Fertile land bordering on the Nile in Cairo today. When the great river flooded, its waters lapped just under the plateau on which the Pyramids stood. The modern city sprawls on both sides of the Nile, with bridges providing links. In ancient times there were no bridges. The only way to cross the river then was by boat.

The Nile was also Egypt's main highway. Boats of all kinds teemed up and down its great length. Then specially-cut canals led away from it to places like Giza. During the Fourth **Dynasty** a canal ran along the foot of the **plateau**, just below where the valley temples were built (see map on page 29). **Wharves** and piers provided places for strong cedar-wood boats to dock. There they unloaded slabs of limestone from just east of the Nile or blocks of red **granite** from Aswan. Then the builders set to work.

Boats played a big part in ancient Egyptian everyday life – for travel, for trade and also for fighting. The men in this **bas-relief** boat are engaged in a battle with an enemy crew. But Egyptian life was usually more peaceful. The deserts and the Mediterranean Sea were good protective barriers for the million or so people inside the **Old Kingdom**, since they were difficult for enemies to cross. There was not even a word in their language that meant the same as our word 'war'.

This **bas-relief** decorates a tomb wall in the cemetery west of the Great Pyramid. The **peasant** farmers are tilling the earth with wooden hoes before planting grain. Men like these helped build the Pyramids during the season of 'akhet' when their land was too flooded to work on. Later the Greek historian Herodotus (about 484 BC to about 430 BC) claimed that gangs of 100,000 men took 20 years to build the Great Pyramid. Modern experts think about 4000 skilled labourers worked at the site all year round, living in special 'pyramid cities' and receiving generous amounts of food and drink.

Sunbeams made of stone

The first known pyramids in Egypt did not have smooth, sheer sides. A famous 'Step Pyramid' at Saqqarah, built before the three at Giza, looked like a great wedding cake. It was made up of six rectangular layers, one set upon the other. The dead **pharaoh**, Djoser, was supposed to use it like a monumental stairway to heaven. And there, in the realm of the sun and sky, he would take his place among the gods of ancient Egypt.

Khufu, Khafre and Menkaure, the pharaohs entombed at Giza, were not expected to climb upwards so **literally**. Maybe their spirits were meant to soar up the smooth sides to the skies. Many experts believe the pyramids themselves were built to look like rays of sunshine breaking through the clouds. Perhaps their summits were once covered in gold to resemble the bright sun.

Mighty monarchs

Whatever shape a pharaoh ordered his tomb to be, his subjects had to build it for him. (In **hieroglyphic** language, the same symbol stood for 'to hear' and 'to obey'. In other words, a subject only had to hear a command and he carried it out at once.) The first pharaoh was said to have been the god Horus. His successors were believed to be semi-

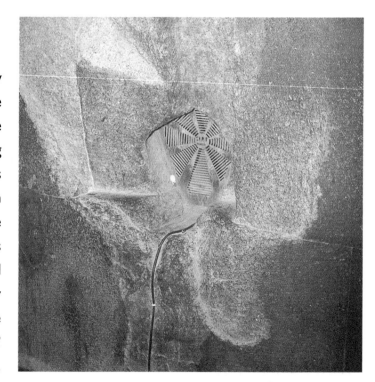

This is one of two openings – now protected by a metal grille – in the wall of the King's Chamber in the Great Pyramid. Each leads to a long shaft that ends at the pyramid's outer surface – one on the north face, one on the southern. Were these used to let air into the King's Chamber? Or were they **aligned** with major stars in the night sky above? If so, did the pyramids have some **astronomical** importance? We cannot be sure.

divine too. A text from the **Middle Kingdom** claimed that 'Ra [the sun god] has placed the king in the land of the living forever and ever, to judge humankind and satisfy the gods, to do Good and destroy Evil.'

Individual pharaohs had varying reputations. Khufu was remembered as a brutal ruler. According to legend, he once had a man's head cut off to see if his magician could re-attach it. He, Khafre and Menkaure all ruled from palaces at their capital Memphis, 24 kilometres south of Giza. From there they could watch their own tombs slowly take shape.

This enormous statue shows the head of a pharaoh of the New Kingdom, Ramses II. It stands in Luxor, Southern Egypt. Few images of Old Kingdom pharaohs have survived.

Ancient Egypt remains a mystery in many ways. But some secrets were unlocked in AD 1822 when French scholar Jean-Francois Champollion managed to 'de-code' the hieroglyphic writings on so many tomb walls at Giza. Some hieroglyphic 'ideograms' or signs depict the things being described; some represent sounds. Around 2000 BC, writers on stone or **papyrus** were using around 700 different ideograms. Ancient Egyptian words that have come into the English language include ebony, gum, sack and oasis.

Putting up a pyramid

The Pyramids at Giza have stood for almost 5000 years. Sadly no evidence on *how* they were built has survived. **Bas-reliefs** show many aspects of ordinary daily life. But building a pyramid was hardly an everyday event. Therefore we have to guess how they came into being, based on our knowledge of other Egyptian building techniques and of the tools Egyptian builders used.

The role of ramps

Before the ground was levelled and foundations were laid, each pyramid's position was precisely worked out. Planners made calculations in relation to the stars and to any other pyramids nearby. Its four sides were then **aligned** with the four compass points. It is quite easy to imagine how the lower blocks were laid. But how were huge stones, weighing 2.5 tonnes on average, raised to the pyramid's higher levels?

A bas-relief from another holy Egyptian site showing a worker preparing unfired brick using small wooden moulds. Although the Pyramids are masterpieces of precision-building, the workers used only the simplest tools. Hammers, wooden mallets, bronze and copper chisels, stone picks with wooden handles and basic measuring instruments have all been found near the Pyramids.

Historians have never agreed on what methods were used. Herodotus (an ancient historian) said the builders had 'lifting machines', but there is no evidence for this. Others suggest the limestone blocks were dragged on sledges up a long straight supply ramp – probably made of **unfired** bricks reinforced with palm trunks. Still others claim that an 'encircling' ramp was used – spiralling ever higher as the pyramid grew taller. It would, however, have been very difficult to drag the stones around the pyramid's sharp corners.

When all the blocks were in place, and the faces had been covered in Tura limestone, a special topmost point or 'pyramidion' was fitted. Made of **granite** or **basalt**, Khufu's pyramidion, now missing, weighed about 7 tonnes.

Egyptian architects had a thorough knowledge of mathematics. This enabled them to design the pyramids with amazing precision. Measurements were based on the 'royal cubit', which was 0.524 metres in length. This was divided into seven 'palms', which were in turn divided into four 'fingers'. A document that survives from about 1600 BC contains a series of tricky problems, like this one: 'A pyramid is 93 cubits and one-third high. What is the angle if the height of its face is 140 cubits?' Any ideas?!

This space between the pyramids of Khafre (left) and Menkaure once teemed with thousands of building workers. The ground around them is surprisingly craggy.

The Great Pyramid

We know little about the mighty **Old Kingdom pharaohs** who ordered each of the three pyramids to be built at Giza. The earliest, most northerly and biggest pyramid was the project of Khufu, the son of Sneferu (another royal pyramid-builder elsewhere in the country). When the Greek historian Herodotus wrote about Khufu he called him Cheops. Today, even in Egypt, the ancient pharaoh is still sometimes known by that name.

The 'Great Pyramid' built for King Khufu around 2550 BC. Its ancient name was 'Khufu belongs to the horizon'. At an original height of 146.6 metres, it was the tallest structure ever built until the Eiffel Tower was erected in AD 1889.

Each of the three pyramids was entered from the north. The high, original entrance to Khufu's pyramid had a double vault over it (A). Below it here you can see the entrance used by visitors today (B). It was opened, according to Arab legend, by the Caliph al-Mamum in the 9th century AD.

A massive marvel

Khufu's man-made mountain contains roughly 2,300,000 limestone blocks, weighing a total of about 6,500,000 tonnes. It is now 138.75 metres high, but once it stood almost 7 metres higher – when its topmost point or 'pyramidion' was still in place. In ancient times it also had an outer casing of white limestone from the Tura **quarries** across the River Nile. This would have made it glitter magically under the hot Egyptian sun. Inside the pyramid is a maze of narrow corridors, steep shafts, and unlit chambers. These can still be visited, as long as the visitor is reasonably fit.

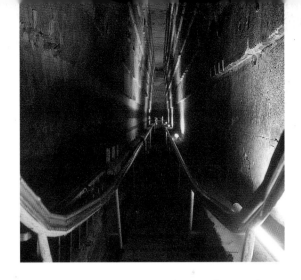

This steep 'Great Gallery' runs for a length of 47 metres right up into the heart of the Great Pyramid – the 'King's Chamber'. It is a masterpiece of construction by the architects and builders of the Old Kingdom.

Here, in the King's Chamber, stands a lidless **granite sarcophagus**. It is slightly larger than the doorway, so it may have been put inside the chamber while the pyramid was still being built. Nothing else is now to be found in the chamber, but many treasures may once have been **looted** from it. An **inscription** left by workmen in an empty space high above the sarcophagus identifies the tomb's owner as Khufu. No other inscriptions have been found elsewhere in the pyramid.

Long after the reign of Khufu, a temple was built just to the east of the Great Pyramid. All that now remains of it are these ruined columns. The temple was dedicated to a goddess known as the 'Lady of the Pyramids'.

A boat for the sky?

To the east and south of Khufu's pyramid there were five deep pits. Each had the shape of a boat – and at least two of the pits had dismantled boats or barges in them. Maybe the other three pits once contained boats too, and were ransacked long ago. Or perhaps they were just meant to **symbolize** boats. Why was this?

We cannot be sure. But the boats and boat shapes probably had an important **ritual** purpose. The Egyptians believed their sun god Ra traversed the skies from east to west every day in the 'boat of the millions of years'. In this way he made sure that day and night happened at the right times. Did the dead Khufu – who was believed to be the son of Ra – possibly need his own boats to navigate the heavens in the **afterlife**?

The reconstructed boat from beside Khufu's pyramid. It is 43.3 metres long, 5.6 metres wide and only 1.5 metres deep. The front of the boat, or 'prow', is carved in the shape of a lotus flower. The back, or 'stern', is shaped like a bundle of **papyrus** reeds. There is no mast for a sail – it is a rowing boat, only for use on rivers or canals.

Remaking the past

Only one of the pits containing a boat has been excavated. (The other boat may already be too damaged to dig out.) Miraculously preserved under gigantic blocks of limestone, the cedarwood vessel was found in 1224 pieces – some only 10 centimetres long. Khufu's name appeared on several pieces, while others had **hieroglyphic** markings that showed how they might be fitted back together. It took over ten years to reconstruct the boat entirely. Today it stands in its own museum, just a short distance from where it was found. All the parts are original except for one oar.

Khufu's 'sky boat' was held together by cleverly knotted ropes, not by nails or metallic parts. Dampened reed mats were also used as a kind of 'air-conditioning' on top of the two cabins.

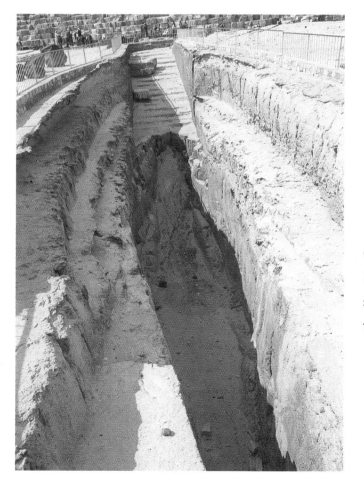

One of the deep 'boat pits' close to Khufu's pyramid. Maybe the dug-out shape was meant to make people think of a boat.

The pyramid of Khafre

The Pyramids at Giza have stood for the best part of 5000 years. Even earthquakes like the one that hit Egypt in AD 1992 have not been able to topple them. But in the course of five millennia, the Pyramids' appearance has changed greatly. They have been damaged by bad weather conditions and by pollution. They have also been **pillaged** by later people, who used the stone to construct mosques and other grand buildings in Cairo.

Most of the connected temples and **causeways** are now in an even worse state of repair. But those attached to the second pyramid are quite well-preserved. By looking at them, we can guess at the religious rituals that were once observed at Giza.

This **diorite** statue of Khafre was found hidden in a well in his valley temple. There were spaces in the temple for over twenty such statues.

This is what remains of the causeway, or 'processional ramp' that runs between Khafre's two temples. It is 494 metres long, and may once have been decorated with sculptures.

Journey to the tomb

The second pyramid was built by the son of King Khufu and Queen Henutsen. His name was Khafre ('Chephren' in Greek). The inside of his pyramid was a lot simpler than that of his father. Some experts believe it had to be built fast. This may have been because Khafre was not young when he came to the throne. The pyramid, temples and causeway all had to be ready for use when he died. But how, exactly, were they used?

It is possible that the dead pharaoh was rowed along a canal to the valley temple to be **mummified**. Then, when the time came for the **pharaoh's** funeral, his body was carried in a procession up the causeway to the **funerary** temple.

Khafre's valley temple is still in very good condition, but we can only guess at what took place inside it.

Funerary temples were built just to the east of each pyramid. This was where the sun rose, or was 'reborn', every day, just as the dead pharaoh hoped to be reborn. Here priests might perform **rites** before the pharaoh was laid to rest in his tomb. Long afterwards **offerings** of food and drink would be left in the temple.

The original name of the second pyramid was 'Khafre is great'. It is now 136.4 metres high. Near its summit we can still see some of the Tura limestone covering that has now been completely stripped from the higher pyramid of Khufu, just to the north-east.

'The Father of Terror'

Over a thousand years after Khufu and Khafre reigned, a prince was hunting in the desert west of Giza. Exhausted, he fell asleep in the shade of a great limestone head near the pyramids. He dreamed that the head spoke to him. It promised the prince that if he freed its stone body from the suffocating sand, he would one day rule all Egypt. So the prince freed the body – and years later he came to the throne as King Thutmose IV.

How do we know this? The story is recorded on a tablet fitted between the freed creature's front paws. Both tablet and creature can still be seen next to Khafre's lower temple. In Arabic the vast statue with its human head and lion's body is called 'Abu Hol' which translates as 'The Father of Terror'. We know it as the Sphinx.

Father-worship?

The Sphinx has always been a mystery. Nothing else like it survives from the ancient world. Most experts think it was built around the same time as Khafre's pyramid **complex**.

It has also been suggested that it is the only remnant of a lost civilization dating back 10,000 years. But there is not a scrap of proof for that!

The much-damaged face of the mysterious Sphinx. It wears a 'nemes' headcloth, a symbol of royalty.

The statue has no **inscriptions** hinting at why it was carved out. But a small temple, now ruined, stands in front of it. Dr Zahi Hawass, Director General of the Giza Pyramids, believes the Sphinx is an image of King Khafre in the shape of Horus, god of kingship and son of Ra. By facing eastwards it is worshipping the rising sun god Ra, who was closely linked with Khafre's father Khufu. So it is possible that while Khafre was still alive, he used his own pyramid complex, including the Sphinx, to worship his dead father. We know for sure that in the **New Kingdom** the Sphinx was known as Horemakhet – 'Horus of the Horizon'.

The Sphinx is about 57 metres long and about 20 metres high. Lion statues 'guarded' the entrances to some Egyptian temples. Maybe the Sphinx was meant to protect the pyramid complex of Khafre behind it.

The arrow points to the 'stela' or stone tablet that records the story of Thutmose IV (about 1400 BC) freeing the Sphinx's body from the sand. Many similar rescue operations have been necessary since ancient times. The Greek historian Herodotus, who wrote in detail about the Pyramids, did not even mention the Sphinx. This was because it stands below the **plateau** on which the pyramids were built, and when Herodotus visited Giza it was completely covered by sand.

Preserving the pharaoh

Pyramids were the final resting places for the bodies of great Egyptian **pharaohs**. The bodies were preserved as '**mummies**', then inside their tombs they were expected to last forever. With the **embalmed** corpses safely stowed away, their spirits would be free to journey on to enjoy eternal life. But not many mummies have survived. Partly this was because in later times tombs were often **looted** for dried mummy flesh, which was sold as a 'cure' for certain ailments.

This is the north face of the smallest of the three Giza Pyramids. Standing 65.5 metres high, its ancient name was 'Menkaure is divine'. The great vertical gash was made some time during the last millennium. The true entrance to the interior can be seen below it.

What happened to Menkaure?

Many rituals accompanied the treatment and entombment of pharaohs like Khufu, Khafre and Khafre's son Menkaure ('Mycerinus' in Greek), the builder of Giza's third pyramid **complex**. The dead man's lungs, liver, stomach and intestines were removed, for example, and put in special 'canopic' jars, so that they would not rot inside the body. The emptied body was dried out and wrapped in long strips of cloth.

The lower third of Menkaure's pyramid was once covered by a layer of red **granite**. Some of it is still there, with limestone slabs covering the rest. Some of the granite blocks were not smoothed down. This suggests that work on this pyramid stopped abruptly – possibly because Menkaure died very suddenly.

Menkaure's body may have been **mummified** in the valley temple at his complex. In his large **funerary** temple there were spaces where his canopic jars were probably stored. His carefully embalmed body may once have been inside the **sarcophagus** discovered in the pyramid's burial chamber in AD 1837. This sarcophagus was lost while being transported by sea to Britain.

Although **archaeologists** have found mummies in many other tombs of ancient Egypt, no human remains have ever been discovered inside a pyramid. Might thieves have stolen them? Or is it possible that some mummies were not actually buried there? We will probably never know the answers.

The smallest pyramid at Giza might look easy to climb. Closer in, the western face becomes far more rugged and challenging.

At Menkaure's valley temple, four striking statues were **excavated** in AD 1908. Each was a **triad** consisting of the pharaoh in the centre, with the horned goddess Hathor on one side and different figures representing the provinces of Egypt on the other.

City of the dead

When a great **pharaoh** like Khufu died, he was reborn to share the throne of heaven with Ra. His relatives, high officials and members of his court then longed to share in the power of his resurrection. So some of them were granted the huge honour of being buried in the shadow of his pyramid. In cemeteries to its east and west, hundreds of private tombs were carefully **aligned** by priests along roads that intersected at right angles. Together they made up a 'necropolis' – a city of the dead.

The strict grid-pattern of the Giza cemeteries was sometimes interrupted when later tombs were built on the same site.

Picturing the past

Egyptian tombs were called '**mastabas**' – which comes from an Arabic word meaning 'stone bench'. From the outside, that is what some of them look like. But inside there might be a deep chamber for the

Seshemnefer IV, an overseer of doctors, was an important official during the early Sixth **Dynasty**. His **restored** tomb under Khufu's pyramid has a far grander **facade** than many of the earlier Giza mastabas. The smaller pictures show the steep 'burial shaft' inside, and Seshemnefer's **sarcophagus** at the bottom of it.

24

burial, with decorated rooms above it where **offerings** could be left. There might also be a sealed cellar containing a life-sized statue of the dead person. This statue was believed to 'communicate' with the outside world through a small crack in front of it.

The mastabas' **bas-relief** decorations give us a vivid picture of the dead person's funeral and lifetime. Scenes might show banquets, parties, life in the country, or the work of artists and craftsmen. Often the dead person, accompanied by close family, is shown supervising all the activities. **Hieroglyphs** tell us who the person was, and what position he or she held under the **pharaoh**.

This slab inside the tomb of Idu – a very high-ranking scribe during the Sixth Dynasty – is a 'false door'. Many mastabas had these 'doors' which did not open, but connected the worlds of the dead and the living. The dead person's 'ka' or spirit was meant to pass through it from the burial chamber, and enjoy any offerings left for him. The figure here – shaven to show he is a holy official – is Idu himself, his hands already upturned to receive offerings.

The birth of a calf, inside the Fifth Dynasty tomb of the high official Iymery.

These **high-relief** statues show Qar (far right) a powerful official during the Sixth Dynasty, with members of his family. One of the figures may be Idu, whose own tomb lies next to Qar's. Some historians believe they were son and father.

A rt for eternity

Some of the art at Giza is quite breathtaking, but ancient Egyptian artists did not set out simply to create works of beauty. In **hieroglyphic** writing, the same symbol (depicting a metal tool for cutting stone vases) stood for both artists and manual workers. At Giza they did not just represent human life – they aimed to use their skills to make life last for ever.

Some of the tomb statues and painted **reliefs** are amazingly lifelike. Their makers hoped that by making them look so real in their sacred resting-places, the dead person might become **immortal**. 'The message of the Egyptians,' writes modern historian Guillemette Andreu, 'who were concerned above all with eternity, has come down through the ages and reached us.'

Qar, an important Sixth **Dynasty** official, was laid to rest in a very elegant tomb. This statue was meant to follow him into the **afterlife** as his exact double. The ancient Egyptian words for sculptor were 'fashioner of life'. When a statue was finished, a priest would perform a ritual called the Opening of the Mouth on it, 'giving' it the five vital senses. The person's name and titles would also be inscribed in hieroglyphs on the statue's base or back pillar, forever merging the actual person and the stone one.

Hieroglyphs were not always written in the same direction, therefore only experts can decipher some of them. These hieroglyphs at the tomb of Idu were made by a technique called 'sunk-relief'. Just the stone within the symbols was hollowed out.

Modest masters of their craft

Architects, sculptors, painters and draftsmen all learned their crafts in special training studios. Sometimes modern art historians can tell the style of one studio from another. But unlike today, artists did not put a **signature** to their works. They did not seek fame for themselves, just eternal life for the men whose tombs they decorated.

Yet we know the name of one artist from the **Middle Kingdom** – Irtysen. His proud son set up a tablet claiming that Irtysen knew how to show, 'the movement of a man who goes, as well as a woman who comes, the panic of a bird caught in a trap, the enthusiasm of one who clubs a lone prisoner, when his eye watches the one opposite him and the face of the enemy is distorted by fear.' He also knew how to show 'the lifting of the arm of one who kills a hippopotamus.' So did many other brilliant Egyptian artists and craftsmen – and the evidence is still there for us to enjoy today.

This **bas-relief** in the tomb of Iymery was painted in **tempera**. A painter's palette was made of six to eight cups, with colours taken from natural sources. White was extracted from chalk, black from charcoal. They were diluted with water then mixed with egg-white to make them easy to apply. Colours on reliefs and statues could have symbolic meanings too, like red for violence and green for youth.

Timeline

Lack of evidence means that most dates are only **approximate**.

c.2925–2575 BC	Early Dynastic period. Upper and Lower Egypt united in to one kingdom. First, Second and Third Dynasties of **pharaohs**. **Hieroglyphic** writing invented.
c.2575–2130 BC	Old Kingdom. Beginning of the Age of Pyramid-building.
c.2700–2625 BC	Capital at Memphis. Reign of Djoser. Step Pyramid built at Saqqarah.
c.2575–2465 BC	Fourth Dynasty. Reigns of Sneferu, Khufu, Djedefre, Khafre, Menkaure and Shepseskaf. Pyramid **complexes** built at Giza.
c.2465–2325 BC	Fifth Dynasty. Reigns of Userkaf and Izezi.
c.2325–2150 BC	Sixth Dynasty. Reigns of Weni, Pepy I and Pepy II.
c.2150–2130 BC	Seventh and Eighth Dynasties.
c.2130–1938 BC	First Intermediate Period. Ninth to Eleventh Dynasties. No pharaoh effectively controls all Egypt.
c.1938–1630 BC	Middle Kingdom. Egypt re-unified, with capital at Thebes. Twelfth and Thirteenth Dynasties. End of the Age of Pyramid-building.
c.1630–1540 BC	Second Intermediate Period. Asiatic immigrants, the Hyskos, control Egypt.
c.1540–1075 BC	New Kingdom. Rule of the Hyskos overthrown. Egypt builds great Middle Eastern and African empire. New capital set up at El-Amarna. Reign of Tutankhamun.
c.935–31 BC	Period of rule by Libyans, Ethiopians, Persians, Macedonians, Greeks, then Romans.

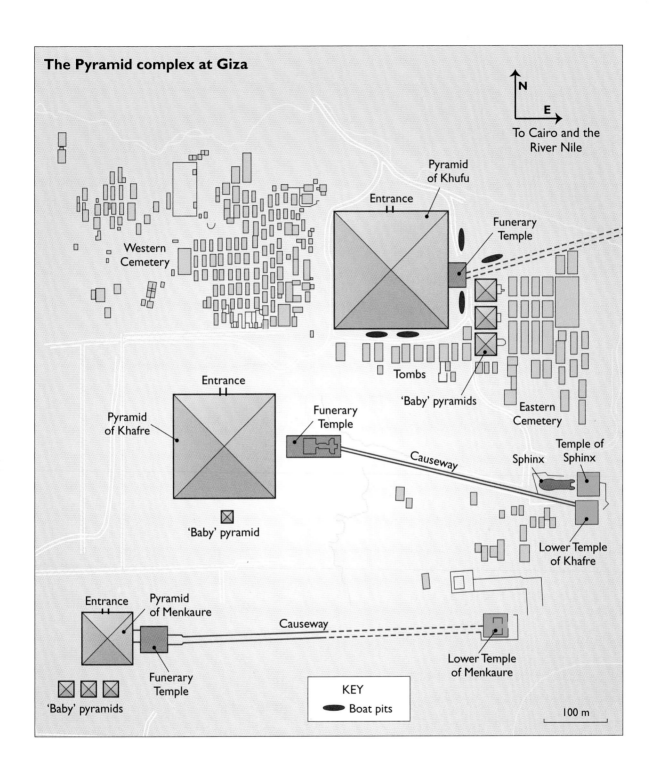

The Pyramid complex at Giza

N
E
To Cairo and the River Nile

Western Cemetery

Pyramid of Khufu

Entrance

Funerary Temple

'Baby' pyramids

Tombs

Eastern Cemetery

Entrance

Pyramid of Khafre

Funerary Temple

Causeway

Sphinx

Temple of Sphinx

Lower Temple of Khafre

'Baby' pyramid

Entrance

Pyramid of Menkaure

Causeway

Lower Temple of Menkaure

Funerary Temple

'Baby' pyramids

KEY

Boat pits

100 m

Glossary

afterlife life after death that ancient Egyptians believed in

aligned lined up with (so that the stars could be seen)

approximate not completely correct

archaeologist someone who studies the past, by looking at the things ancient peoples left behind, like buildings and pottery

arid very dry, with little rain

astronomical to do with studying the stars and other heavenly bodies

basalt dark volcanic rock

bas-relief carvings where the design stands out a little way from the material being carved

causeway raised-up road

complex related group of buildings

diorite speckled kind of stone

divine like a god or goddess, superhuman

dynasty series of rulers, usually related to each other

embalm preserve (a body) by being treated with chemicals

excavated dug up by archaeologists

facade front of a building

faced covered with another material

fertile suitable for growing crops

flax a plant with fibres that can be woven and seeds that give oil

funerary to do with funerals and burials

granite very hard rock

hieroglyph ancient Egyptian form of writing, where pictures represent both sounds and words

high-relief designs that stand out further than bas-relief

immortal living forever, like a god

inscription words inscribed on stones or coins

literally in actual fact, taking words at their face value

loot to steal or seize

mastaba simple bench-like tomb

Middle Kingdom period of Egyptian history running from about 1938 BC to 1600 BC

mummify preserve by drying out and embalming

mummy body of a dead person specially treated to stop it decaying

New Kingdom period of Egyptian history running from about 1540 BC to 1075 BC

offerings gifts left in a person's honour

Old Kingdom period of Egyptian history running from about 2575 BC to 2130 BC

papyrus material from an Egyptian plant. After being treated, it was used for writing on.

peasant ordinary country worker

pharaoh ruler of ancient Egypt. The pyramids were the tombs of pharaohs.

pillaged stolen, plundered

plateau area of fairly level high ground

quarry place where stone for building can be obtained

reliefs carvings that stand out from the background surface

restored repaired

rites/rituals traditional religious services

sarcophagus stone coffin

signature autograph

symbolize represent, stand for

tempera type of painting in which egg yolks are used to spread the colours

triad group of three connected people or things

unfired not baked in a kiln

vault large space or chamber

wharves places for boats to be tied to, then loaded or unloaded

Index